D1530428

TEEN HOT LINE

GANGS

Debra Goldentyer

RSVP
RAINTREE
STECK-VAUGHN
PUBLISHERS
The Steck-Vaughn Company

Austin, Texas
1994

302.34
GOL

Consultants:
Gerald C. Ronan, Director of Professional Services, Family Service Association of Bucks County, PA
Kenneth J. Schmidt, Senior Probation Officer, Probation Division, Passaic County, NJ

Developed for Steck-Vaughn Company by Visual Education Corporation, Princeton, New Jersey
Project Director: Jewel Moulthrop
Editors: Dale Anderson, Paula McGuire
Editorial Assistant: Carol Ciaston
Photo Research: Cindy Cappa

Raintree Steck-Vaughn Publishers staff
Editor: Gina Kulch
Project Manager: Joyce Spicer
Electronic Production: Scott Melcer
Photo Editor: Margie Foster

Library of Congress Cataloging-in-Publication Data
Goldentyer, Debra, 1960-
    Gangs / Debra Goldentyer.
        p.   cm. — (Teen hot line)
    Includes bibliographical references and index.
    Summary: Discusses why kids join gangs, gang life and activities, related drugs and violence, getting out and staying out of gangs, and where to go for help.
    ISBN:0-8114-3527-X
    1. Gangs — United States — Juvenile literature.   [1. Gangs.]   I. Title.
II. Series.
    HV6439.U50645   1994
    302.3'4—dc20
                                                          93-1427
                                                          CIP   AC

Printed and bound in the United States

2 3 4 5 6 7 8 9 0 LB 99 98 97 96 95 94

CONTENTS

What the
Teen
Hot Line
Is All About

This book is like a telephone hot line. It answers questions about gangs that may puzzle you. Answering them requires us to give you the facts. You can use those facts to make your own decision about joining a gang. So think of us as the voice on the phone, always there to answer your questions, even the ones that are hard to ask.

Just so you know where we stand, here is a list of steps that we think every person should take before deciding to join a gang. They focus on using common sense and finding out facts. They assume that you want to make your own decisions and that you want to behave responsibly toward both yourself and your community.

1 Find out everything you can about gangs in your neighborhood and in other neighborhoods.

2 Talk to others to get information you need—your parents, your friends, your teachers.

3 Separate your own feelings about joining a gang from the pressure you may be feeling from others.

4 Think about what you expect to gain from being a gang member and consider whether there are alternatives that may be better for you.

5 Decide whether or not you want to join a gang and let others know your decision.

6 If you decide not to join a gang, stay away from gangs and their activities and find friends who have made the same decision.

After reading this book, we hope you will have some answers to your questions—and perhaps to some questions you hadn't thought of yet. In the back of the book is a list of sources for further information. Thinking about the issues raised in this book is an important step toward taking control of your life.

Interview

Maria joined the local gang and began using drugs at age 13. At 21, she gave birth to a son. Because of her drug use, her baby was taken away from her. Eventually, she was able to turn her life around. Now 28, Maria has been married one year. Her second child, a girl, was born three months ago. She hopes to get custody of her son in the coming year. While no one story is typical, Maria's story tells what gang membership can do to a teen's life.

Getting into the gang was easy. You just have to be bad, you know what I'm saying? You just have to be accepted. You have to have that kind of mentality that, you know, that you're cool. 'Cause if you're like a wimp or something, they'll slap you around. But if you're more, like bold and cool . . . you get accepted.

I was about, maybe twelve, thirteen years old when I just started out. Because before that, like I was going to ballet school, tap dancing—I was, like, a good girl. But then the peer pressure—you know, I wanted to hang out; I wanted to be accepted.

I've got one sister, two brothers, and my mom. . . . My father died of alcohol and drug overdose when I was ten.

My mom, she had to support the family. . . . She was a IBM keypunch operator. . . . Then she started having nervous breakdowns, and then she got on welfare.

I grew up in a lot of projects. I lived in about five projects. . . . My mom tried to get us out, you know, but nothing was open but the projects. . . . But when I hit Army Street project, things started getting really bad.

We had our first little gang. It was called Garfield Mafia, 'cause Garfield Park was right across the street . . . and we were a mafia. . . . It was a mixed gang 'cause there was a lot of blacks there, too. But that was hard for me, too, because not being black, I had to fight a lot to be accepted.

I started getting high, going out, and just experimenting into drugs—drinking beer, getting drunk. You know, just experimenting. . . . I smoked a lot of PCP[angel dust].

I was trying to go to school. I would get into a school and then think I would make it—you know, I wanted to go to school—that was my thing. But . . . I always got involved in peer pressures, getting high, and that was it.

I was just remembering this incident where we were in this house with this bunch of Samoan* dudes. These guys were real crazy, and we just started hitting them upside the head with skates, I mean, it was real crazy. And there were times when I fought this guy and hit him with a baseball bat, and I fell down the stairs. We were at this party. . . . I guess he wanted to throw us out. . . . We were all drunk, and we started rolling down the stairs, and he hit me with a crowbar. Then . . . some dudes that I knew from another gang . . . came with baseball bats . . . and started fighting him.

*Samoans are people from the Pacific South Seas Islands.

Once in a while we'd rob a house here and there or just steal or just . . . rob people of their money. . . . But I haven't done nothing really, uh—I got busted for assault and battery one time, though. Oh, I did steal a car . . . and I got busted for assault and battery for beating up these two girls, me and my friend. So they threw us in jail, 'cause we really beat them up real bad, put them in the hospital, and knocked their teeth out.

Oh yeah, I stabbed one guy. For my sister. Well, we was messing with these Mexican dudes. I didn't think I stabbed him. . . . As I stabbed him, I didn't feel nothing. 'Cause I guess when you stab somebody, you don't feel it. But that's just something—I'm not proud of it, but when I go back and I remember, it's kind of heavy. I really did all this, not realizing that I was hurting somebody.

And then I went to a halfway house. . . . I got kicked out of there 'cause I tried to hit somebody in the head.

I thought I could get it together. So I started working and doing, you know, a couple of jobs here and there. And then I moved back to the projects, and I started doing crack. . . . It was real easy to get. At first it was cool, 'cause everybody was partying, you know. So that's when everything started hitting the fan.

When I was 21, I had a baby boy, but he got taken away when he was a little baby 'cause I had drugs in my system. . . . They took him away for about two weeks. But I got him back. But they took him away again 'cause I was doing crack.

If you're into drugs . . . it's real hard to have a relationship with your child 'cause your mind is not on your child. Your mind is on getting high. There were times when I'd have my child with me, and I didn't even notice him. I would get high. I would tell him to go in the other room. It's not your fault—I can't explain it.

The worst thing that can happen to a girl is . . . getting "tossed out." That means selling your body for drugs—not for money, but for a hit. Where I lived at the end, I would see girls actually . . . go into a room just for a hit of crack and do something with the guy. I would see this, and I knew if I didn't get out, I was going to be like that.

They were selling their body for a hit—I can understand, if you want to make some money, but for a hit? Uh-uh. That's crazy. But it happens.

The worst thing about being in a gang is, I think, being hurt by your friends. I mean being backstabbed. That was heavy. When you're close to somebody and you're in a gang, and they backstab you. That happens a lot.

If somebody got some drugs and maybe you got none, they'll leave you. You know what I'm saying? You'll get high with them first, and then somebody else will walk in—you know, just getting burnt. Then you start to realize that these people don't care about you. You know, they don't care about you—they just want your money, and when the drugs are all gone, later, to the next one. That's another thing. A masquerade, you know—a mask that people put on their faces, and it's not real. 'Cause when they're in jail—like if I was in jail, who's going to come see me? Who's going to send me money? Nobody! Nobody! My mother, probably, but nobody else.

People in the gang were phony. People didn't really accept you for who you were. They didn't love—you know, they just weren't real. They're just hateful. They didn't care about nothing. I seen people just slap people in the face like there's no kind of love in them. See, there's still love in my heart. And it would hurt me to see somebody get hurt. At the end, I knew there was something for me. This wasn't my destination.

People think it's fun out there—and it's not, man, 'cause it'll catch up to you sooner or later. It will. And it's real serious. They think it's a joke to be hip, to be bad, to be cool, but that ain't where it's at.

A lot of my friends are dead. A lot of my homeboys [neighborhood friends] are dead. . . . A lot of them—I have a lot of friends that are dead now. They died from PCP, hanging theirself, drownings, jumping off the bridge, shooting, being on the freeway, getting hit by a truck and split in half, just things that if I didn't straighten up, I'd probably be right along with them.

I wasted a lot of my life being in a gang. I could have gone to college. . . . I could have a degree; I could be working, you know, making good money, having a nice house. But see, I wasted my life—on what? What? Nothing—just hanging out and trying to be bad.

BULLETIN BOARD

Age of Gang Members
Percent of gang members under 25: 96%
Percent of gang members between 12 and 21: 90%
Average age of gang members: 17
Average age of gang members who kill: 20

Numbers of Gang Members
Estimated number of youth gangs: 120,000
Estimated number of youth gang members: 1.5 million
Gang sizes: any number, up to hundreds of members
Number of teenage boys in large cities in gangs: 1 in 5

Crime Among Gang Members
Children under age 18 arrested for murder in 1991: 2,674
Children arrested for violent crimes in 1991: 114,200
Number of children killed in violent crimes in 1991: 2,771
Percent of high school students in 1989 who carried a gun: 4%
Percent of students in 1989 reporting gangs in school: 15%
Percent in 1989 reporting gang fights in school once a week: 12%
Approximate number of teenagers killed every day: 7
Number of white boys killed in 1988: 9 in 100,000
Number of black boys killed in 1988: 83 in 100,000
Number of white girls killed in 1988: 4 in 100,000
Number of black girls killed in 1988: 16 in 100,000

Ethnic Breakdown of Gangs

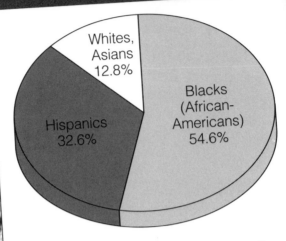

Whites, Asians 12.8%

Hispanics 32.6%

Blacks (African-Americans) 54.6%

Source: Spergel, Irving, et al., *Survey of Youth Gang Problems and Programs in 45 Cities and 6 Sites*, University of Chicago, 1990.

Teens in Jail (1989)

Number of white teenagers in public juvenile detention facilities: 22,200
Number of black teenagers in public juvenile detention facilities: 23,800
Number of Latino teenagers in public juvenile detention facilities: 8,700
Average age of teenagers living in juvenile detention facilities: 16

Sources: Grinney, Ellen Heath. *Delinquency and Criminal Behavior*. Chelsea House, 1992.
Office of Juvenile Justice and Delinquency Program 1991 Annual Report. U.S. Department of Justice, 1991.
Simons, Janet M., Belva Finlay, and Alice Yang. *The Adolescent and Young Adult Fact Book*. Children's Defense Fund, 1991.
Snyder, Thomas D. *Youth Indicators 1991*. U.S. Department of Education, 1991.
Statistical Abstracts of the United States, 1992. U.S. Department of Commerce.

CHAPTER 1

Communicating

Q My name's Malcolm and I'm 14. My friends are putting pressure on me to join the neighborhood gang, but my big brother says he'll kill me if I do. Who should I listen to? How can I decide what to do?

A Teens face a lot of pressure from many people. Your parents pressure you to behave, your teachers pressure you to do well in school, and your friends pressure you about nearly everything. But if you do things just because someone tells you to do them, how good are you going to feel about yourself? When it comes to making important decisions like this one, you have to learn to satisfy yourself first.

• • • • • • • • • • •

A Before you can make a decision, you need some facts. Have you asked your friends why they want you to join the gang?

Q No, but I've got all the facts I need. Being in a gang is fun, it's cool, you get respect from other kids, and you've got friends who'll always be there.

• • • • • • • • • • •

A And have you asked your brother why he doesn't want you to join the gang?

Q Well, no. But he'd probably say that it's dangerous, that I could get hurt.

• • • • • • • • • • •

A So, who's right?

Q I don't know.

A It sounds as if you need some more information before you make your decision. You might want to start with your brother. Ask him if he can sit down with you and talk—alone, just the two of you, brother to brother. Tell him you want to know why he doesn't want you to join the gang.

• • • • • • • • • • •

Q Yeah, well, my brother's always being too protective of me. He's going to tell me all these scary stories. Maybe they're true, maybe they're not.

A Okay, but listen to what he says with an open mind. Then check up on the stories. Talk with your friends who want you to join the gang. Ask them what the gang does. Ask if anyone in the gang has been arrested or hurt and how that happened.

• • • • • • • • • • •

Q I already know what they're going to tell me—there's no way to survive in this neighborhood unless you're in the gang.

A Is that really true? How did your brother survive? Look

A school counselor will be able to advise you about the consequences of your decision and to guide you to other sources of information.

around—perhaps there's an adult in your neighborhood whom you respect—a teacher, a minister, or someone in your family. Sometimes, a youth center or a school has a counseling office that helps young people think through tough decisions like this one. Someone there might even be able to introduce you to a person who once was in the gang. I bet that person could answer a lot of your questions about what it's like to be in a gang.

• • • • • • • • • • • •

Q I suppose. But, come on, the guys'll treat me like a nerd if I don't join them.

A Maybe they will. But if your friends leave you because you decide not to join, what does that say about them?

Anyone who cares would want you to make your own decisions. If these friends don't let you make your own choices, maybe you should have other friends.

• • • • • • • • • • • • •

Remember, this is your decision to make, not your friends' decision. You're learning how to take charge of your own life. The decision you make today could affect the rest of your life. You owe it to yourself to make it carefully.

The best way to make any decision is to get the facts. Maybe you'll decide you do want to join a gang. Maybe you'll decide you don't. Either way, you'll know your decision is informed.

Making Your Decision

Before making your decision, gather all the facts you can. You've probably heard many things about gangs. Perhaps you've heard that being a gang member is cool, that everyone respects gang members, and that gang members have lots of friends. You also may have heard just the opposite—that being in a gang is not cool, that no one respects gang members, and that they're your friends only when they need you. You may have heard that gang members hurt people, get hurt themselves, get arrested, and drop out of school. You may have heard that being in a gang is the only way to survive. And you may have heard that getting out of a gang can be tough. How much of this is really true?

■ First, examine the facts. Learn as much as you can about gangs, what gang members do, and how their actions affect their lives. Don't make a quick decision. Talk to as many people as you can and get as many viewpoints as possible. You might want to read some books or see some videos about gangs. Discover what you'd give up by joining and what you'd give up by not joining. Make a list of the pros and cons of being a gang member and then take a hard look at your list.

■ Second, examine your feelings. Are you thinking of joining because you want to or because your friends want you to? What do you want to be doing in five years or in ten years?

What Is a Gang?

❏ **Definition**
A group of people who associate with each other regularly; sometimes commit antisocial acts; common behavior; reside in same locale; often same ethnic background

❏ **Organization**
Established identity; leadership; goals; membership recruitment and rules; exclusion of nonmembers; affiliations or conflicts with other gangs; control of turf

❏ **Symbols**
Name; colors; rituals; logo; graffiti; initiation; tattoos; clothing; nicknames

❏ **Noncriminal activities**
Protection of selves, group, and community; recreation; sports activities

❏ **Criminal activities**
- Drug crimes: drug use and sales
- Crimes of violence: rape; intimidation; drive-by shootings; robbery
- Property crimes: vandalism; burglary; theft; auto theft

Youth gangs exist throughout the United States. Some deal drugs; others harass ethnic and religious minorities; and some protect their neighborhoods. Teen gangs are not all alike. Yet they do have some common characteristics, as shown on this chart.

Will being a gang member help you meet your goals? What do your instincts tell you?

■ Finally, make your decision.

Communicating Your Decision

Telling others about your decision can be as hard as making your decision, yet it's just as important. Let's say you decide not to join the gang. You must tell your friends what you've decided. Unless you tell them clearly what you've decided, they may not understand that your decision is final. In that case, they may continue to apply pressure on you to join.

Planning the Conversation

Peer pressure sometimes makes people say and do things they don't want to say and do. It's hard to have a meaningful conversation with a friend if either of you feels pressured. For that reason, it's probably easiest to talk with one or two close friends about your decision, rather than the whole group.

Plan in advance what you want to say. You worked hard to make your decision, and you know why you made the choice you did. Plan to share your reasons and be prepared to explain your position clearly. You may want to try out what you're going to say on someone who agrees with you before you talk to the others.

Having the Conversation

Start the conversation by telling your friends how you feel. Tell them that you like and respect them, but you don't feel the same way about the gang as they do. Then tell them what you've decided about the gang.

Give your friends a chance to respond and listen to what they say. Don't argue. The purpose of your conversation is to tell them which decision is right for you, not to convince them that you are right or they are wrong. Leave it to each of them to make their own decisions about what's right for them.

If you tell your friends you don't want to join, they may threaten to stop being your friends. You already know that is one of the risks of your decision, and you must be prepared to accept it. They may become angry and insistent. If so, it will be important for you to make it clear that you've made your decision and intend to stick by it. They will have to decide what they want to do about it.

Still, your friends may surprise you. Sometimes when you communicate your feelings and worries with friends, you find they share many of the same feelings. If your friends haven't yet joined the gang, or even if they have, they may have doubts about whether joining is right for them. They may welcome the chance to talk about those doubts. This may be an opportunity for you to lead and gain respect from your peers.

Many teenagers base their decisions on what they believe others are doing. Sometimes it seems that everyone else in school belongs to a gang. The truth is that most young people are not gang members. If it looks as if they are, that's because gang members tend to receive an excessive amount of attention because they make so much trouble.

Sticking to Your Decision

Once you've made your decision and explained it clearly to your friends, there are some situations that you need to be prepared for.

■ Don't let someone talk you out of your decision. You can change your mind, but only if you decide to.

■ Don't send mixed messages. Be consistent. Choose to be in the gang or out. If you appear to be in sometimes and out sometimes, you will have problems.

■ Don't put yourself in situations that might make it hard for you to stick to your decision. Don't spend time with the gang if you're not a part of it. Spend your time with other friends and stay as far away from the gang as you can.

No matter what you decide to do, making the decision by yourself is one of the first steps in taking control of your life. Because this is a difficult decision to make, line up some support for yourself—someone you trust and respect who supports your decision. Practice how you're going to communicate your decision to the others. When you feel ready, tell the others. Then return to your support person for some positive reinforcement after explaining your decision. You don't have to be alone!

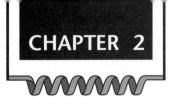
Why Kids Join Gangs

Q My name is Duc. My family moved to the United States from Vietnam two years ago. American kids tease me and make fun of the way I talk. My brother says the only way to survive is to join a Vietnamese gang. Is he right?

A Nothing is more important to a teenager than having friends and fitting in. Yet that's especially difficult for you, since many of your classmates see you as "different." You may look different, the way you speak is different, and you have a history that is very different from the others in your school. All these differences are bound to make things difficult for you.

• • • • • • • • • • • •

Like everyone else, you'd like to have someone to talk to about the difficulties you face, and someone to turn to when you are insulted or harassed. When you were younger, you may have relied on your parents for support. Yet now, new to America, your parents are facing problems of their own. Many young people who are new to this country find that their parents, as much as they want to help, really can't do much more than tell them to figure things out for themselves.

Since many of your American classmates won't accept you and your parents can't help you, you turn to others like yourself—other Vietnamese or immigrant kids. They understand you, they offer you their support and advice, and they offer you safety in numbers if other teenagers get a little rough and want to start a fight with you.

It is important for teenagers—American or immigrant—to be part of a group. Spending time with peers is a very important part of growing up. The big question to ask yourself is whether you have to join a gang to get the friendship, support, and protection you need.

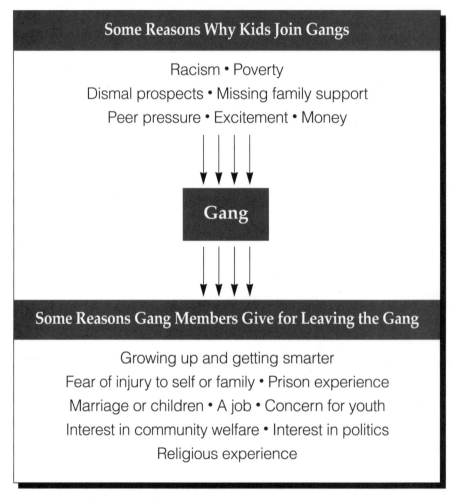

Some Reasons Why Kids Join Gangs

Racism • Poverty
Dismal prospects • Missing family support
Peer pressure • Excitement • Money

Gang

Some Reasons Gang Members Give for Leaving the Gang

Growing up and getting smarter
Fear of injury to self or family • Prison experience
Marriage or children • A job • Concern for youth
Interest in community welfare • Interest in politics
Religious experience

Young people join gangs for many reasons. But as gang members grow up, marry, and have families of their own, many begin to worry about their own kids growing up in violent neighborhoods.

Duc is like many other young people who grow up in gang neighborhoods. But it's not just immigrant teenagers who are drawn to gangs. Many young people—American-born and immigrant, rich and poor, urban and rural—find something appealing about being a gang member.

Who Joins Gangs and Why

What is it that makes kids join gangs? Let's look at some of the reasons.

Racism

Duc, in his question, mentioned one reason for joining gangs: racism. Many people—adults and teens alike—fear or hate people who are different from them. For new immigrants to this country, like Duc and his family, language barriers and cultural differences make life difficult. Immigrants tend to band together with people of similar backgrounds for mutual support and survival. But when they exclude others, or are excluded by others, trouble begins.

This separation is dangerous, especially for young people. Fear and hatred often escalate, and teens who know little about one another except for those of their own race, begin to attack one another.

Poverty

For kids growing up in poor neighborhoods, gangs can appear especially attractive. If you are too young to have a job, or if you are old enough but no one will hire you, what do you do? What's there to do after school, on weekends, or during the summer?

Jamal joined a gang for these reasons. He lived in a poor neighborhood. There was nothing for him and his friends to do. There was no youth center, no gym, no shopping mall, not even a pizza place. Even if there had been a movie theater, a pool, or a skating rink nearby, he couldn't afford to go there.

Jamal and his friends just hung out on street corners, looking for some way to pass the time. In time, some tougher kids, who turned out to be gang members, invited them to help them. They were going to rob a store and if Jamal and his friends would play "lookout," they could earn a little money. Jamal's boredom, coupled with the opportunity to earn some spending money, led him straight into the hands of gang members.

Dismal Prospects

Some families have lived in poverty for generations. Children from these families may feel that they don't have a chance of doing better than their parents. For those who have little hope of a better future, joining a gang may seem like a good idea.

In addition, many young people feel angry about their lives. They feel that they are denied access to good jobs. They feel that they've been cheated and have only one another to depend on. They act out their resentment by joining gangs and attacking society and one another.

Missing Family Support

Everybody needs the support of a loving family—people who know you, people you can go to when things go wrong, people who will drop everything when you need help with a problem. Unfortunately, many young people can't rely on their own families for that support. In the 1990s, an increasing number of families are extremely poor. Take Gloria's family, for instance. Both her parents have to work long hours in order to feed her and her brothers. Her dad has two jobs and her mom makes what money she can by cleaning people's houses. They have little time to be with Gloria or help her with problems.

In her neighborhood, Gloria is better off than many of her friends—she has two parents and both of them have jobs. Others have only a mother. And some of the mothers have no jobs—and no money for the family.

Teens your own age who have had similar experiences can frequently offer you support by means of local peer counseling groups.

Being out of work, or working at a low-paying job, is depressing and often lowers an adult's self-esteem. Yet, times are bad and many people have been in this situation for months or even years. They are struggling to keep everyone fed, and they don't see that things will change anytime soon.

Some parents reach such levels of despair that they start using drugs or alcohol. Others take their frustrations out on their children. Neither is the sort of parent a child can, or wants to, rely on.

When parents are struggling to survive, they can't provide much help to their kids. Young people are often left to fend for themselves, with little supervision or care. Some teens feel that they have to raise themselves and often their younger brothers and sisters as well.

Frequently there is a "safety net" for young people who are without family support. In some neighborhoods, a church or community center may offer support services, such as peer counseling or Alateen (a program for teenagers of alcoholic parents). Groups such as Role Models, Unlimited, in Seattle, and Big Brothers/Big Sisters throughout the country connect young people with older people who want to help. Quite often, the older person is a former gang member who wants to help teenagers avoid the mistakes he or she made.

Without a supportive family or community, many young people seek out the support of street gangs. For them, gangs serve as a sort of substitute family and support network. (In many cases, gangs truly are families, as older relatives may also have joined the gang.)

Peer Pressure

Peer pressure is probably the biggest reason teenagers join gangs. Pressure from peers to join a gang is not unique to poor or minority neighborhoods—it's all over America. According to law enforcement agencies, even middle-class and wealthy teens join gangs. When it appears that "everyone" is in the gang and when your friends pressure you to join, it can be pretty difficult to say no. Your friends really want you to be part of it. They coax; they argue; they tease you for being afraid or immature. And most likely, if you don't join, they won't be your friends anymore.

It's normal to want to go along with the crowd. Each of us wants to be accepted and liked by the people around us. When most of your friends began to use certain phrases, cut their hair in a new style, or began wearing a particular item of clothing, didn't you want to do the same? Perhaps you have even done something that you didn't really want to do, just to go along with the crowd.

What Can a Kid Do?

Doing things you don't want to do may be a large part of being a gang member. Before you join a gang, consider what you may be required to do. Fellow gang members may expect you to steal, to hurt someone, or to sell or use drugs.

You have to ask yourself whether this is what you really want to do. Are these the kinds of friends you want, or are you better off making new friends?

There may not be much you can do right now to change your family's financial situation or to make your parents pay more attention to you. However, if you want a future for yourself and your community, you may want to look seriously at the alternatives to gang membership, such as community groups, school athletics, or a part-time job.

Find Alternatives

There are many safer, noncriminal alternatives to joining a gang. Think about what you'll gain by being a gang member. If it's friendship and support you're after, look around. Are there youth groups, sports teams, or church groups in your neighborhood? Is there a Police Athletic League? What about groups in your school? Joining school clubs or music groups, working

Taking part in after-school activities will give you an opportunity to explore one of the alternatives you may have to develop friendships without joining a gang.

on the school play or newspaper, and starting a band or rap group are good ways to make friends—without committing crimes or hurting other people.

Like Duc, are you thinking of joining a gang for protection? Ask yourself if you are really afraid for your life. Most harassment is probably harmless, and if you can ignore it, it will stop. That may be true in your case. However, in some neighborhoods, gang members don't stop to ask questions. If they don't recognize you as a gang member, or if they think you belong to a rival gang, they attack. If this is the way it is in your neighborhood, you may need help from others to protect yourself. Fortunately, there is help—from other family members, community groups, school counselors, and even the local police department. Almost every police department has someone who has been specially trained to help teens. Check it out!

Help Reduce Gang Activities
You are not going to change your situation overnight. But with help from others, there is much you can do. In most neighborhoods, there are people working to solve the problems caused by racism, poverty, and gangs. In New York City, a group of teens became disgusted with what gangs and crime had done to their neighborhood. They joined Youth Force, an all-teen community group that works to clean up public places such as parks. By organizing nighttime dances and other activities, they made the parks unattractive to gangs and "took them back" for use by the communities. Youth groups, such as this one, offer many of the "benefits" that gangs do—friends, a sense of belonging to a special group, relief from boredom. The difference is that with youth groups, there is hope and a future.

Consider doing similar work rather than joining a gang. By doing so, you can make positive changes. Not only will this make your future safer, it will also improve the lives of your family, your neighbors, and the children who will live in your community in the future.

Gangs and Status

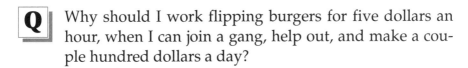

Q Why should I work flipping burgers for five dollars an hour, when I can join a gang, help out, and make a couple hundred dollars a day?

A Making money by joining a gang seems easy, doesn't it? Many gang members sell drugs. Others break into people's homes or rob people on the street. Some more organized gangs force shopkeepers to pay them large sums of money. These criminals can always use someone—especially someone young—to help them by carrying weapons, watching for police, or hiding stolen property. It looks as though there are lots of opportunities for young people to make quick cash by joining gangs and helping with their criminal activities.

It's true that you'd have to flip a lot of burgers to make what you would by helping a gang. But think about it. Nearly every gang activity hurts someone. Do you really want to sell drugs to little kids, or even help someone else sell drugs to little kids?

Remember, too, that all these activities are illegal. If you get caught, you'll be arrested. You may have to spend time in a juvenile detention center. You will almost definitely have a criminal record—and every time you commit a crime, your punishment will become more severe. How is that criminal record going to look when you decide to get a job?

You have to decide whether you are willing to do anything to make money, even if it may destroy the lives of others or destroy your own future.

What Gang Membership Seems to Offer

When asked why they joined a gang, gang members usually mention three primary reasons: money, popularity, and excitement. It's true that membership appears to offer these rewards. Yet, as with many other things in life, appearances can be deceiving. Whatever you get from joining a gang, there is a steep price to pay.

Money

At first glance, it appears that being a gang member can be a good way to get rich quick. Some gang members strut around in expensive jewelry, wearing the latest fashions, and driving fabulous cars. It seems to others that they're doing very well.

That's what Karen thought when she saw the older kids in her neighborhood. She compared her life to theirs. As long as she could remember, her family had been struggling to make ends meet. Karen's dad works seven days a week. He leaves the house before Karen leaves for school, and he comes home as late as ten o'clock at night. Now that her little sister is old enough, Karen's mom works full time, too, and comes home worn out each evening. Yet as hard as they work, Karen notices, they never seem to have enough money. They struggle just to buy groceries, and they aren't buying any jewelry or expensive clothes. How many lifetimes would it take before she could get a winter coat that hadn't belonged to her brother first?

Karen is only 14 years old, so she can't even get a real job. About all she can do is babysit, deliver newspapers, or help around the house. From those jobs, she'll never earn enough to help her family or buy herself a new coat.

But she is old enough to join a gang, or at least to help the gang in its activities. Gangs prefer to use young kids—and don't mind paying them for their help—for several reasons. The main reason is that children are not punished by the law in the same way adults are. The juvenile court system doesn't

A 13-year-old drug dealer, protected by his snarling dog, drops exhausted after a night of dealing drugs on the street.

send young children to jail and is often more lenient than the adult system. Also, the police are usually less suspicious of the activities of a kid than those of an older teen. Finally, by using kids to carry weapons or hide drugs, gang members know they are protecting themselves from being arrested. In return for their help, younger kids and younger gang members get money, valuables, or drugs—all for doing work that's much easier than housework or looking after someone's baby.

For some, gang membership—and the money it offers—may seem necessary to survive. In families with only one parent, there is often pressure on the oldest kids to help out. If they can bring in money by serving as a lookout, at least it helps mom.

The trouble is, there is a steep price to pay for the "easy" money. Once you join a gang and get involved in its crimes, it's hard to get out. Some kids figure they'll "play it safe" by working with the gang for a couple of months, make some money, then quit before they hurt people or get caught by the police.

Unfortunately, few get involved in crimes without also getting arrested or hurt, and few can turn their lives around easily when they decide they've had enough. After you've done a few jobs for the gang, they expect you to do more and more dangerous ones, until you're in too deep and can't get out.

Where does this leave you? If you're like Karen and most other teens, you want to make some money—for yourself or to help out the family. It's true that a young person really can't make a lot of money. The best way you can help yourself and your family is to accept that fact. Think of your first job as just that—your first job. Work hard at it, get some experience, and soon you should be able to move into a better job.

Of course, that's a slow process, especially compared to the quick money you can make on the streets. But what kind of career do you think criminal activities will prepare you for? How long do you think you can go on selling drugs or robbing people? It's hard to be an active gang member and stay in school, and it's hard to get a job if you don't stay in school. Also, it's much harder to get a job once you have a police record.

Popularity
Many kids think that being a gang member wins them popularity and respect. By hanging out with a large, tough group, they certainly command a lot of attention. Sadly, they may not realize that others are looking at them not with respect or admiration, but with fear and dislike.

You can be sure you'll have friends and be popular when you join a gang. But that "friendship" will be tested regularly. To prove your loyalty, you may be asked to do anything, including fighting and killing.

Usually, the only people who are impressed by gang members are other gang members. If you're like most people, you're impressed by people who have self-confidence, look like they will get somewhere, and can do so without hurting others.

Does being tough really make you feel popular? Or does it

just mean that you're a bully who doesn't care about anyone but yourself and your friends?

Excitement

When you hear about gangs on television or read about them in the newspaper, you may think gang members lead exciting lives. That's what made Leon join a gang—he found life as a teenager to be dull. He was too old to do the childish things his parents let him do and, according to his parents, too young to do many things he really wanted to do.

So he joined a gang and found it exciting. He was constantly being challenged. He was attacked nearly once a week by rival gangs. He was stopped regularly by the police. Even his fellow gang members provoked him. They made him prove how tough he was, how much he could get away with, how badly he could beat up others, and how much pain he could take. He was always on the edge of adventure—about to get beaten up, arrested, maybe even killed. It wasn't long before he realized that this wasn't the kind of excitement he'd had in mind.

Being a gang member is never a part-time situation. You have to be prepared always. You have to be on guard because you never know when you will be challenged or attacked.

Some kids join gangs simply because they feel it's exciting to do something they shouldn't. Some join because they want more attention from their parents. This is one reason rich kids join gangs that steal—they know they could ask their parents for anything they want, but they find stealing more exciting.

Gaining independence from parents is an important part of being a teen. Every healthy teen is something of a rebel. In fact, many deliberately do things their parents don't want them to do. The trick is to be a rebel in a way that doesn't jeopardize your future. Take a few chances—but before you do, consider the consequences of your actions. If what you're planning to do may hurt someone, ruin your future, or get you in trouble with the police, maybe you need to think of something else to do.

What Gang Membership Really Offers

Wanting to have money, popularity, and excitement isn't unusual or bad. But despite appearances, joining a gang doesn't really offer these things. What little it does offer comes with a big price tag.

Even though you might make some money, you're bound to get involved in criminal activities. You are likely to have a criminal record and probably some serious physical injuries. And you're likely to spend time stealing from, hurting, and scaring people.

You might be popular, but only among those who think that being a member of a gang is a good idea. Other people are less likely to be impressed.

As for excitement, if you think undergoing surgery to have a bullet removed is exciting, then you're all set. If you want to know how many blows you can endure before you fall into a coma, you may like gang fights. If you want to be afraid to go out on the streets because a rival gang or the police are looking for you, then you'll enjoy gang membership.

It seems like a lot to risk for what little you get, doesn't it?

Because of the availability of sophisticated weapons, gang crimes have become more violent. These teenagers were arrested after a shooting in a New York City pool hall that killed one person and injured several others.

CHAPTER 4

Gang Activities

Q My name's Aida. My boyfriend, Fernando, was a member of the Demons. Last Saturday night, he was shot and killed by a member of another gang. Why did he have to die? Why do gangs fight each other?

A Gangs fight for many reasons, and most gang fights end in permanent injury or death. The fights are often about what most people would consider small matters. For example, a gang member is likely to be beaten for walking down a street that's "claimed" by a rival gang. A guy might be attacked by three or four others because he was seen talking to a girl who—he finds out later—is the girlfriend of a rival gang member. Or a gang member may be shot simply because someone thought he or she had not shown the proper respect for another gang member.

• • • • • • • • • • • •

In many cases, gang warfare—and it is a war—starts out small and grows. Almost all gangs are violent. When gangs begin to fight, each attack gets more violent than the last. Gang fights usually result in someone's death. That may have been how Fernando died. Death among gang members has become so common that many who join gangs expect they won't live very long. They accept that as a fact of life, as a price for the way they live.

What Do Gangs Fight About?

Most gang activity is criminal, and most of the crimes involve some sort of violence. Much—but hardly all—of the violence is between members of rival gangs. Most fights erupt over turf disagreements, long-term feuds, or racial hatred. Some fights start just because a gang member wants to show off his or her strength or toughness.

Turf

A gang's "turf" is the area that the gang claims as its own. The term usually refers to a geographical area, such as a certain neighborhood, street, or housing project. It may refer to an area—such as a particular junior high school—where that gang claims the exclusive right to sell drugs or the exclusive right to commit other crimes. For example, some Asian-American gangs prey on Asian-American businesses and families and will fight anyone from a different ethnic background who does the same. The names of many gangs come from the name of their turf, such as the Broad Street Bloods or the Southsiders.

Gangs usually use graffiti to define and establish their turf. By writing their names on the walls of the area, gang members declare—mostly to other gang members—that everyone within that area is subject to their gang's rules. Any rival gang member who sets foot in or drives through that turf may be beaten or even killed. The controlling gang rarely stops to find out the rival gang member's reason for being there.

Turf lines are rigidly enforced. Once a gang's turf is defined, gang members stay as close as possible to it and rarely venture into another gang's turf. One gang member who had been doing well in school had to drop out when he joined the gang. He said he couldn't get to classes without crossing the turf of a rival gang—and doing that was far too dangerous.

Jerry had a fatal turf story to tell. Jerry, a member of the Killers, needed something from a particular store. Since he knew that the store was in an area that "belonged" to another gang, the Korea Boys, Jerry tried to get in and out as quickly as he could. "I blew it," he explained later. "Choon, one of the Korea boys, saw me in there. He busted me pretty bad."

Jerry went back home and told his gang what had happened. He and four others went after Choon for revenge. They found him and beat him up. "The Korea Boys came back after us with knives, so we had to fight fire with fire." Before long, both the Killers and the Korea Boys were using guns. Within a short time, several members of each gang had died in the "war."

Feuds

A lot of gang violence stems from long-established rivalries between two gangs. Often gang members don't even know why they are fighting. The Bloods and the Crips are two rival gangs that started in Los Angeles in the 1970s. Although these two gangs have much in common, each has identified the other gang as the enemy. Few, if any, current members of the Bloods or the Crips know why the other gang is the enemy or what started the feud. But gang members on both sides will fight to the death for the honor of their group.

Like those of the Bloods and the Crips, feuds between many gangs have lasted several generations. Those who started them are long dead or out of the gang. All the current gang members know is that the other gang is the enemy and it is their duty to protect the neighborhood from them.

Racial Hatred

Sometimes gang warfare grows out of racial prejudice. Gangs are usually composed of particular ethnic groups. For example, there are Chinese gangs, African-American gangs, Mexican gangs, Native American gangs, Irish gangs, Samoan gangs, and Korean gangs. Although not all gangs are segregated in this way, those that are often find themselves in the middle of racial fighting.

There are many kinds of gangs, and they exist for different reasons. Skinheads originated in Great Britain in the 1960s and consisted of mainly tough, angry young people from working-class families. There are groups now in the United States and in other countries. Because of their racial and religious bigotry, they are considered a neo-Nazi group.

Some gangs are even formed for the purpose of committing hate crimes. For example, skinhead gangs are usually made up of white youths whose main purpose is to promote white supremacy and bigotry against people of color, Jewish people, and various other groups.

Show of Strength

Gang members like to show others, especially other gang members, how much power they have. They need to prove themselves and establish a reputation as people "no one can mess with."

One way gang members prove themselves within their own gang is to commit a particularly gruesome crime. One way to prove themselves with rival gangs is to hurt them more than they've been hurt. That's why each revenge attack is deadlier than the last.

Other Crimes Gangs Commit

Criminal activity of gangs goes well beyond warfare between gangs. Gang members also steal, sell drugs—often to young children—and terrorize their neighborhoods.

Theft

Gang members spend a lot of time trying to get rich. Some break into homes; some steal cars. Some attack people on the street, taking their money and valuables. Working as a group, gangs can be very effective—and very violent.

More and more gangs today are learning from adults and older gang members how to commit organized crimes. They learn to terrorize neighborhood businesses, forcing them to make regular payoffs of large sums of money. These payoffs are called "protection" money, because gang members protect the business owner from getting beaten or killed.

One of the most frightening crimes gangs have learned to

commit is the home invasion. A group of members commit this crime by breaking into a house or apartment in their neighborhood when the residents are home. Once inside, they steal everything they can and often torture the victims.

Drug Dealing

Many gangs are involved in selling drugs, especially crack, which is a powerful, extremely addictive form of cocaine. Often, drug dealers will approach young children and let them try a drug once or twice "for free." Soon, the children are addicted and must pay the dealer to continue their habit.

The large profit that can be made from drug dealing has resulted in gangs spreading out beyond their turf. Gangs are even moving into areas that never had gangs before. In these new areas, the gang members find many "new customers" for drugs. One Kansas official said that "when the heat's on from police in bigger cities around the country, the gangs reach out to other communities."

Vandalism

Some gangs, especially those made up of younger kids, are unlikely to break into homes or sell drugs. Instead, they engage in mischief. Their crimes start small, such as marking up walls or breaking windows in abandoned buildings. They may do these things because they think it's fun or because they're bored and have nothing else to do.

Often, as gang members grow tired of these minor acts, they move on to worse crimes. They may start by damaging houses and cars and later move on to more serious violence, such as "wilding."

Wilding

"Wilding" means cruising in a pack, looking for someone to beat up or rape, just for excitement. In one well-publicized incident, a gang of teenagers—thought of by their parents as "good kids"—roamed through Central Park in New York City. They beat and kicked the people they encountered. One female jogger was knifed, beaten, raped, and left for dead. By the time she was found, she had lost three quarters of her blood and had to be hospitalized for seven months. The boys later explained they had attacked people because they were looking for "something to do."

Stopping Gang Crime

If there are gangs in your neighborhood, there is probably vandalism, drug dealing, theft, and violence. You can't stop any of these criminal acts overnight, but you can work with your community to reduce gang activity.

Stopping the Violence

Gangs gain their strength through numbers. In the same way, you can fight back through numbers. By not joining a gang, you are slowing the growth of their numbers and strength. Getting involved with others in the community to put an end to gang activity is an even more positive step. Find out from the police, your teachers, the churches, and community groups what is being done to reduce gang activity. Then ask how you can help.

In a group of housing projects in Chicago, for example, gang members and other teenagers are invited to compete with each other in a midnight basketball league. Competing on a basketball court has reduced competition on the streets. It might work in your neighborhood, too. Check with the local police, school, church, or community center to see if they can help you to start a similar program in your area.

Preventing Theft

One of the best ways to prevent theft in your community is through a neighborhood watch program. Neighbors keep an

Helping to Reduce Gang Activities

These are some of the strategies being used with the community as a whole or with individual gang members.

Community Organization	❑ Cleaning up the community (neighborhood cleanup and beautification programs) ❑ Mobilizing the community (Neighborhood Watch) ❑ Improved communication with official organizations
Social Intervention	❑ Youth outreach and street counseling ❑ Referrals for services ❑ Counseling of gang members ❑ Recreational and sports activities ❑ Temporary shelter ❑ Helping members leave gang ❑ Changing values of youth to make gang involvement less likely
Opportunities	❑ Job training and placement ❑ Assistance with school ❑ Teaching of basic skills; tutoring
Suppression	❑ Arrest, imprisonment, supervision, rehabilitation
Organizational Development	❑ Special law enforcement units ❑ Special youth agency crisis programs ❑ Local governments and agencies creating, modifying, or expanding special units to deal with gang problems

Source: Spergel, Irving, et al. *Survey of Youth Gang Problems and Programs in 45 Cities and 6 Sites,* University of Chicago, 1990.

Government, community groups, schools, and law enforcement agencies are working to reduce and eventually eliminate gang activity.

eye on what's going on and report suspicious activities to the police. Watching out for one another can make everyone safer. If your community doesn't have a neighborhood watch program, ask the police how you can help them start one.

Stopping Drug Activity

Former drug addicts and people who have treated addicts agree that the best solution to the drug problem is prevention—teaching kids not to take drugs before dealers have a chance to get them to start.

If your neighborhood doesn't have a drug prevention program, see who is interested in starting one. Since drug dealers try to sell drugs to young children, direct your efforts toward getting to those kids first. Perhaps there are after-school programs, summer programs, and other wholesome activities that you can help with.

Cleaning up Graffiti

Gangs use graffiti to mark off turf, and turf battles are one of the major causes of death and injury in many communities. If your neighborhood is marked with graffiti, it may be a target for violence.

With the help of a minister, community leader, or other concerned adult, you can reduce the risk of violence by organizing a neighborhood graffiti clean-up campaign. Enlist community members to go around the neighborhood regularly and paint over graffiti as soon as it appears. In some areas, city maintenance offices may help by offering the paint, brushes, and ladders. The sooner you can get the graffiti off the walls, the safer you can make your neighborhood. However, this action may also be dangerous. By informing the local police department about your clean-up campaign, you can probably avoid any revenge violence by the gang whose graffiti you are trying to cover up.

Life in a Gang

Q When my friend Carlos joined a gang, he told me about this horrible initiation he had to "survive" first. Was he telling the truth, or did he make the whole thing up just to seem tough?

A He was probably telling you the truth. Many gangs make people who want to join go through a test or initiation, sometimes called a "jumping in." Jumping in is often a painful process.

• • • • • • • • • • • •

Gangs don't want anyone who isn't tough or who won't be loyal. They also want their new members to know who's in charge—and who's at the bottom of the ladder. If you want to join a gang, you might have to prick yourself with a pin and take a blood oath. You might have to get a certain kind of tattoo. Some gangs' jumping-in ceremonies include such rituals as drinking chicken blood. Girls who want to join a gang often are raped as part of their jumping in. Very often gangs stage organized beatings of new members, sometimes beating new members until they are hurt so badly that they can't get up.

Gang members take membership very seriously. They see joining a gang as permanent. To impress this on new members, they often require some sort of permanent marking of membership. In one gang, each new member's arm is cut with a knife in a way that it forms a scar with a particular shape. One gang requires members to be burned with cigarettes on the back of

Obtaining tattoos is frequently a requirement for gang member identification, but tattoos may be impossible to remove if you don't want them later in life.

their hands. In another gang, new members must cut off a tip of a finger when they join. In this way, once new members go through the jumping in, everyone they meet later in life will know that they had once joined a gang.

Becoming a Gang Member

Gang "wannabes"—people who want to join gangs—often must prove to the gang members that they have a useful talent or that they are worthy. They may be required to steal a car, set a fire, win a fight against one or several gang members, or even shoot someone, either a rival or a random victim. Some gangs call this "earning your stripes." Some gangs require only one act to earn stripes. Others make "wannabes" go through a long testing period.

"By the time I was 14," Jacob remembers, "I wanted to join a gang. I hung out with gang members. I learned how they dressed, and dressed just like them. I spent a lot of time trying to show off to them." To impress the gang, Jacob made home-made weapons. He made a riot stick—the kind the police carry—out of an old metal bedpost. He made knives out of wood and plastic so that the gang members could get weapons past the metal detectors at the school entrances. "Honcho—the leader—was finally impressed. He'd let me in, he said." But, as final proof, Honcho told Jacob that he had to shoot a member of a rival gang. "By that time, I had already worked so hard to impress Honcho that one last act—shooting someone—wasn't as hard as I'd expected it to be."

Being a Gang Member

Being in a gang, or almost any group for that matter, requires a certain amount of conformity, that is, behaving as the group behaves. Certain characteristics distinguish teen gangs from other youth groups.

Colors

The first characteristic most people notice about gangs is that the members dress alike. Although it's not true of all gangs, many do wear the same sort of clothes or the same color of clothes. They do this so that they stand out as gang members. Dressing alike is also an unspoken warning to others who might want to attack a member. Outsiders can see by the number of people dressed alike that the person they're thinking of beating up has strong protection.

Some gangs wear their clothes in distinctive ways. They might cock their hats to one side, turn a pocket inside out, cuff their pants a certain way, pierce one ear, or wear one glove. Tattoos and unusual hair styles are also common identifiers.

In many areas, each gang chooses a color that identifies that gang. In Minneapolis, for example, the Vice Lords wear black and gold. Their rivals, the Disciples, wear blue and black. Nearly everything the Vice Lords wear—shirts, bandannas, shoelaces, caps—is black and gold. If they have tattoos, they are black and gold. Some even paint their fingernails to match. Equally important, nothing they wear is blue. Wearing blue would get them beaten up—either by members of the Disciples for wearing their color, or by other Vice Lords, for disloyalty.

Graffiti

Remember that gangs use graffiti to mark off their turf and to issue warnings and challenges to rival gangs. All gang members can read gang graffiti. They usually react immediately if they don't like what they see.

For example, the Barrio Boys had marked off their turf by writing the name of their gang on the walls of a church. Their rival gang, the Eastenders, painted a slash through the graffiti. Both gangs knew that the slash was a challenge from the Eastenders to fight for the turf. Within hours, the two gangs were battling. By the end of the fight, two Barrio Boys were hospitalized and one Eastender was dead.

Many gangs stake out their turf by painting graffiti—street names and gang logos—in playgrounds and on walls in their neighborhoods. Crossing out or painting over a rival gang's graffiti is considered a challenge to fight.

That's another way gangs use graffiti—they often paint elaborate, colorful memorials to fellow members who died "in action."

Hand Signs and Language
In addition to dress and graffiti, gangs use hand signs. By flashing these signs to each other, gangs can identify themselves even if they don't wear the same colors.

Some gang members have even changed their use of language to honor their gangs. The Los Angeles Crips, for example, are the rivals of the Bloods. Many Crips will not use the letter "b" in their speech and members of the Bloods will not use the letter "c."

Street Names
New gang members are given a moniker or street name. All others in the gang will call them by that name rather than their real name. The name may reflect a personal characteristic ("Shorty") or a particular crime or ability ("Little Speedy"). The most important reason to have a moniker is for protection. If gang members don't use their real names, it will be harder for the police to find them. Remember, gang members are always avoiding the police.

Life in the Gang

In some ways, it sounds exciting to be a gang member, doesn't it? It's like being in a secret club, doing dangerous things, and having a group of strong and loyal friends to back you up. Before you join a gang, though, you need to know what life in a gang is really like.

Rules of the Gang
Some gangs are loosely organized groups of kids who hang out and cause trouble. Others are very strictly run, just like

businesses. There is a leader, there are high officials, and there are regular gang members who try to work their way to higher positions by committing crimes and impressing the leader. There may even be older "veterans" who oversee the gang's activities.

Many gangs have strict rules of behavior—and strict disciplinary actions for any member who breaks a rule. Some gangs have designated a single person to be the enforcer of the rules. The enforcer, often the strongest person in the gang, keeps all the other members in line. Most enforcers believe in quick and painful punishment for any member who violates one of the gangs rules.

Probably the most important rule in any gang is that members can't say no. When you're told to do something, you must do it. If a fellow gang member gets beaten, you must repay that beating. If your gang wants you to sell crack to elementary school children, you must do it. If you don't do what you're told, you're considered disloyal. Anyone who is disloyal can expect to undergo the most serious punishment.

In effect, you give up your personal freedom when you join a gang. Probably the greatest act of disloyalty is to try to leave the gang. Gang members are taught early on that the needs of the gang are more important than the needs of any individual member. Many gang members say the only way to get out of a gang is to die.

Drugs
At some point, gang members realized that large amounts of money could be made by dealing drugs. Many gang members do not use drugs themselves, because they know what using drugs can do to them. Drugs interfere with brain functions and render people unreliable. People who use drugs can't be depended upon in a fight. If you're counting on your friends to protect you in a gang dispute or during a gang action, you don't want them to be high on drugs.

Even though they realize that drug use has serious consequences, not all gang members have been able to resist drugs. Many are addicted—most commonly to crack cocaine, heroin, or PCP. Gang members say that the fun of taking drugs wears out quickly when they see what happens to their friends—and to their friendships. When you run out of drugs, they say, you run out of friends.

Using drugs makes people not only unreliable and stupid but violent. Much is said about loyalty between gang members, but that loyalty often has its limits when it comes to drugs. Many gang fights are between members of the same gang—about a minor misunderstanding that was blown out of proportion because the fighters were high.

Recruiting New Members

Gang membership may look exciting, but it turns out to be truly ugly. For this reason gangs recruit very young kids, some as young as eight or nine years old. Children are attracted mostly by the outward excitement—the colors, the hand signs,

Younger children often admire older gang members, and are drawn into the gangs as a result.

the graffiti, and the drugs—but don't see the down side. Many young people don't understand the commitment—often a lifetime commitment—that they make when they do join a gang. They're not aware of the many things they'll have to do once they're in.

Many gangs encourage young people to join by having a young "clique," or "set." The younger group often has a name, such as the Midgets, the Juniors, or the Peewees. Members of these groups usually don't have to go through any sort of vicious jumping in, but they are expected to help the older teens. If they do what they're told, and show some willingness to participate in criminal activities, they may be given the honor of joining the older gang when they become 12 or 13.

The younger sets can be very useful to gangs, especially gangs involved in drug-related crimes. Young children are often asked to carry drugs or weapons because they are treated much more leniently by the law if caught. For example, an adult or an older teen who is caught selling drugs may have to spend at least two years in prison. A child, on the other hand, may spend only a short time in a juvenile detention facility.

Girls in the Gang

Most gang members are male. Gangs have traditionally used girls, as they've used little children, to help them with their criminal activities. Girls were useful because the police were less suspicious of them. Girls could stand on street corners and serve as decoys while boys committed robberies. Girls could hide weapons or drugs in their clothes, knowing that the police would be less likely to frisk them.

Gang members often treated girls as gang property, like guns or knives. Passed along from gang member to gang member, they were never allowed to be gang members themselves.

Today there are a number of girl gangs, and some male gangs permit girls to be members. Girl gangs and girls in gangs are becoming more and more violent. Police no longer

Some teenage girls have their own gangs; but most female gang members serve as support for male gangs. Traditionally, girls were used to conceal weapons and drugs because the police were less likely to search them.

look the other way when they see girls loitering. And police are not reluctant to frisk girls who they feel may be involved in illegal activities.

Bretta and her friends started their own gang because they felt they were being treated unequally by the guys in their gang. "When my homegirls and I started the Lady Locas, the guys in the 12th Street Gang laughed," Bretta said. "One guy told me we were too cute to be tough. We weren't going to take that stuff. We attacked them one night and smashed them pretty bad. They don't call us cute anymore."

So that's what gang life is all about—violence, fear, drugs, and pain. The initiation often gives new members a taste of gang life, but by the time they realize what they're in for, they're already members—often for a lifetime.

Interview

Marcus is 17 years old. He joined a gang when he was 13. Two years later, after a number of arrests and four detentions in a juvenile facility, he became disillusioned with gang life. With the help of friends and religion, he managed to turn his life around. Today he works as a youth minister for a church dedicated to helping others who want to leave gang life. While no one gang experience is typical, Marcus's story is about someone who was able to turn his life around.

I grew up in a real poor family. My mom was on welfare all my life, and we really never had much. But as soon as I got to the age of maybe 10 years old, 11 years old, I was interested in my cousins and my uncles who were involved in gangs. I used to see what they used to do. For instance, I had a cousin who used to smoke PCP. . . . He used to jump out of trees, and he used to act like he was Superman and stuff. I used to look at him, and I used to like him. I used to say, "That's what I want to be." . . . That was my role model.

I was born in the neighborhood, so it was natural that I was going to hang around with the people in the neighborhood. Everybody in the neighborhood, we were one gang—we were called the Mitchell Street Gangsters. I lived right there on Mitchell Street. And there was about 19 or 20 of us.

I was, like, 13 when I started hanging out . . . having

fun—partying. Like what we would do every Saturday night is we would go and we would cruise around the boulevards and we would look for any gang member that was by himself. And I remember one time we went to this fast food place and there was one—he was from another gang. He was there by himself, and there was about 20 of us. . . . And we jumped out the car and we started beating him up in front of his girlfriend, and his girlfriend started screaming, and we threw soda in her face—it was just fun.

Fighting with the other gang started out a long time before I got in the gang. What happened was, the leader of my gang, he never got along with them in the first place. One time he smashed a crowbar through one of their heads, and all kinds of stuff like that. But what he would do is . . . he would plant a seed in us not to like them.

He was 22 years old, and he had already been in the gang probably about ten years or something. Anyway, he would encourage us, like "Don't worry about anything." Because at one point the gang started getting smaller—people started going to jail. We had two homeboys that got locked up; they were doing seven years each for killing somebody—he would encourage us and tell us, "Don't worry about it." . . . He would say, "Don't ever let nobody get you down; somos pocos pero locos"—in Spanish that means, "there's not many of us, but we're crazy."

I got kicked out of school when I was 15 for probation violation. 'Cause I had already been to jail four times. . . .

At that point I was trying to stay out of trouble by just, you know, trying to prevent trouble from coming my way. But what happened was another gang member, he came and hit me. And I had a knife on me, but I didn't want to stab him because I knew the consequences. So I started to walk away, and he figured that I was going to go tell. I mean, he figured that I was going to get him after school with my knife or something—or I was going to get the rest of my friends, my homeboys. So what he did, he went and told on me—that I had a knife. So the police came and took me to jail. And that was it.

The first time I was arrested was for jumping an Asian guy. . . . The second time, I went for strong-armed robbery. The third time, I had two charges—I had joy-riding and I had strong-armed robbery again. And then the fourth time was violation of probation.

It was just for the fun. Like the third time, what we did is we beat up a lady. She was real drunk, and we took her car, and we laughed about it.

To get new kids to join the gang, we'd introduce them to drugs. . . . The youngest guy, he was 12 years old. We called him Little Capone because he was 12 and he was real big. By the age of 13, he was already doing heroin. And he went through rehab and came out still doing it.

The way that we would initiate people is we would beat them up, and we would tell them pass by your neighborhood, and they would have to shoot somebody, stab somebody, or do crazy things like that. They didn't have to really kill them, but just—damage them.

I was one of the guys really that made the younger kids do something. . . . I would tell them to run in the store, grab liquor, and run out—stuff like that.

There was a couple of guys in the neighborhood that weren't in the gang; they were nerds. We would go in their houses and take their parents' jewelry and stuff like that. We'd lock them in the garage and stuff like that.

There's probably about four ways to get out of a gang. Either you die, you go to jail, you move away, or you get saved.

I was in juvenile hall, and I was telling God, "If there's any way out of this—help me." See, I grew up in a real religious family where you go to church on Sunday. . . . So anyway, what happened was, I would tell God, "Get me out of here, Lord. I'll try to get out of the gang life."

Even now I get tempted to get back in once in a while, but. . . . I think back and I see it's not worth it.

I've got four tattoos—I got them all when I was 14 years old. (Laughs.) I wish I could erase them, but—it's too late now.

It's not worth it, none of it. It all ends up in prison or death, one or the other. Even if you do make it out, there's still no future in being in a gang.

CHAPTER 6

Gangs and the Community

Q I'm Carla. I'm scared all the time. The gangs around here are pretty violent, and I'm afraid I'm going to get killed by a stray bullet or something. What can I do?

A Gang activities can get very rough in some neighborhoods. If there are gangs in your area, you have good reason to be afraid. Even if they are only fighting each other, gang members' fights often affect innocent bystanders.

• • • • • • • • • • • •

The best thing to do is to play it safe. Don't try to be a hero and stand up to gangs. Don't confront them. Don't show them that you're scared or that you're impressed. Have as little as possible to do with gangs. As much as you're able, ignore and avoid them.

Don't meet with friends where gangs do. If the gangs in your neighborhood like to meet in the parks or near a convenience store, go somewhere else with your friends.

Many schools now have a youth gang officer to monitor gang activities in the school. These officers have been very helpful in reducing crime and protecting young people like you, who want nothing to do with gang activities. If you're ever scared, find the officer and ask for help.

If you see gang activities in your neighborhood, report them to the police. Don't do anything else. Stay away from the gang and say nothing to the gang members. Try not to draw any attention to yourself. Report what you see and let the police handle the situation.

Work with adults in your community to take positive action. Many communities have taken a number of steps to fight gang activities. You could join a community graffiti cleanup group. Since gangs need graffiti to show off, mark turf, and leave messages for each other, removing it helps prevent gang conflicts. Neighborhood cleanups and community pride programs help chase gangs away.

You may want to become a teen peer counselor, helping others your age stay safe. You may want to get involved in local political issues, such as improving the schools, getting better police protection, or helping revive your neighborhood. Tell community leaders that you're interested in helping and you'll see how many others are working to improve your community. It will be a great feeling.

What Gangs Do to Communities

Whenever a gang forms in a community, that community is likely to suffer. This is especially sad, since most gang members operate in their own neighborhoods. Through their activities, they hurt the very people who care most about them.

Crimes Against the Community
Some gangs spend a lot of time trying to get rich. Members of these gangs may mug people on the street. They may break into homes and businesses when no one is there, or force their way inside and terrorize those who are there. In a new type of crime called "carjacking," gang members steal a person's car by threatening the driver with a weapon. Sometimes gang members set fires or destroy property they've robbed just for excitement.

Residents of gang-infested communities often live in fear. Threatened by gang activities, many literally live behind bars—steel bars that they've put on their windows and doors. They leave their homes only when they have to. They travel only in groups and almost never go out at night. Many parents in these areas won't let their children play in public parks.

Many people in these neighborhoods choose to carry guns or knives. Yet, carrying a weapon often does nothing to increase security. Increasing the number of weapons in an area simply increases the probability of injury and death.

When gang members use drugs, violence in the community usually increases. When they need more drugs, addicts are willing to do almost anything to get them. They become desperate, and some drugs make users more aggressive. People who use drugs often can't think rationally. They lose any fear of injury or jail. They become much more likely to attack people in public areas, and they often inflict serious injuries.

Violence Among Gang Members

Gang violence occurs most often between gangs or between members of the same gang. It is usually not directed toward the local community. Even so, everyone in the community is a potential victim. You may be in danger even in your own home.

One of the latest, and most deadly, forms of violence among gang members is the drive-by shooting. In a drive-by shooting, gang members drive through another gang's turf sometimes carrying powerful military-type weapons. Because these guns can spray a wide area with bullets very rapidly, gang members believe they will hit their targets. Unfortunately, they are also likely to wound or kill small children and other bystanders.

When Marcos drove into the Warlords' turf to take revenge on his rival Juan, he found him in a parked car. Marcos shot ten bullets into the car, managing to injure Juan seriously. However, one of those bullets killed a neighbor taking out the trash. Another blinded an 11-year-old girl at home watching television.

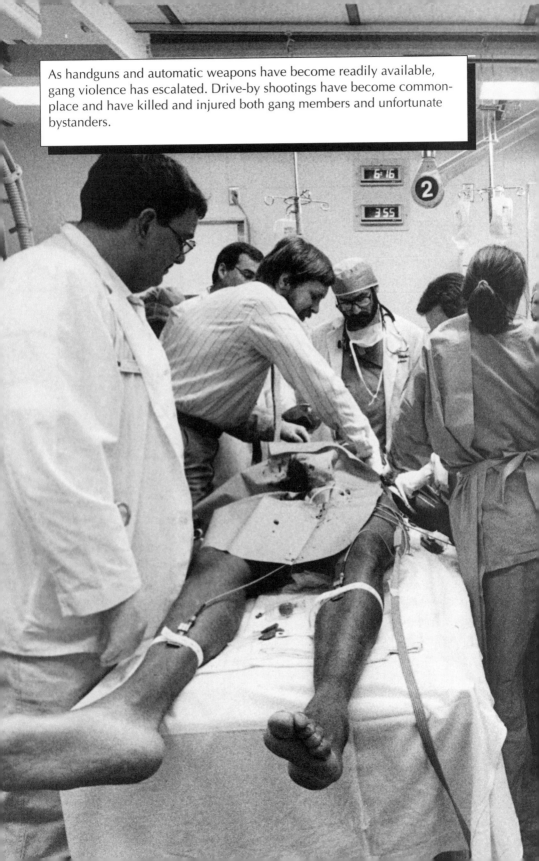

As handguns and automatic weapons have become readily available, gang violence has escalated. Drive-by shootings have become commonplace and have killed and injured both gang members and unfortunate bystanders.

Windows don't stop bullets. In areas where drive-by shootings take place, many people have learned to live their lives "low." They sit on the floor. They sleep on the floor. In this way they are well below the level of the window and less likely to be hit by a bullet.

Drug Sales

Violence is not the only way in which gangs hurt communities. Gang members often sell drugs, and many people are willing to buy them. By supporting community members' drug habits, gang members weaken the whole community.

Gang members don't limit themselves to supplying existing drug users. They are always looking for new customers. After all, the more drugs they sell, the more money they make. And the more customers they find, the more they can sell.

Their favorite places to look for new customers are the elementary and junior high schools. Younger children are more likely to believe what older teenagers tell them. Many young children haven't yet understood the message about what drugs really do to their lives. And many find it very hard to say no.

Bringing in New Members

Gang members also turn to elementary and junior high schools for new members. Since so many gang members are killed or in jail—and since most gangs depend on numbers for their strength—gangs always need more members.

Gang members know how to attract little children. "We watch for kids who are impressed by how we dress," Zeke explains. "We look for kids who don't have a lot of self-respect—kids who seem to be seeking out a role model, a family, some sort of connection. We never have to say a word to them—they come to us. They see the way we act, how much others are afraid of us, how we're always together, and they want in. And the best part is—they'll do anything we tell them to, for a chance to be let in."

Increasing Community Violence

Gang members believe that the best way to get what they want is through aggressive behavior. In gang life, violence is the way of doing things. If members want money, they mug someone or break into a house. If they are angry at someone, they try to teach that person a lesson with their fists or a knife. Gang organization is based on violence; in many gangs, the leader is the one no one can beat up.

People who learn to use violence are less likely to use other appropriate ways to get what they want. Even after they leave the gang, they are likely to resort to violence. Caryn left her gang when she was 17. She got a job but was often late to work. When her boss fired her, Caryn was so angry that she pushed him down a flight of stairs and broke his arm.

Caryn knows no other way to deal with her anger. Now she has a baby, and when he cries, she hits him. Growing up around Caryn, the baby will probably learn no better way to deal with his anger. He's likely to resort to violence as he grows up.

How Bad Is It?

How bad has gang warfare become? It has become so serious that the U.S. Army has begun to send doctors to gang neighborhoods for training. These doctors can count on getting round-the-clock experience in how to treat severe injuries such as gunshot wounds—the kind that used to be seen only in military battles.

Families of gang members also live in fear. They worry that the gang member they love may be hurt or killed on the streets. At the same time, they must worry about their own safety. Parents, brothers, sisters, and even cousins and grandparents, may be victims of gang retaliation, even if they have nothing to do with the gang.

Children in gang neighborhoods know the sound of gunshots because they hear it almost every day. They grow up surrounded by drug use, violence, and death. Children grow-ing up under these circumstances often become withdrawn or distressed. They often carry with them a feeling that they have no future and no hope, especially since they're not sure if they're going to duck the next bullet safely.

Gang activities, once confined to the poorest neighborhoods, have moved into richer areas. Gang members know there's not much for them to steal in poor neighborhoods. They also know that rich kids can afford to buy more drugs and pay higher prices than those in poorer neighborhoods. Not only is gang activity worsening, it's spreading.

The situation has become so bad, in fact, that even some cur-rent and former gang members are trying to stop the crime and

Gang violence has reached intolerable levels—even for some gang members. Following the Los Angeles riots of 1992, members of the Crips and the Bloods announced a truce by tying their gang bandannas together to symbolize their common goal—peace in South Central L.A.

the violence. In May 1993, two unusual meetings took place—one in Los Angeles, California, and the other in Kansas City, Missouri. Gang members from several cities gathered to begin "trucing"—calling for peace and setting goals for the future. Their aim is to establish relationships with business leaders and government officials to provide jobs and to help resolve the problems of America's cities.

What Can Be Done

Most gang activities are criminal, and there are federal and state laws against them. The police are doing everything they can to stop gangs and crime, but law enforcement is only part of the solution. You and your community, working together, can do far more.

Help Keep the Neighborhood Safe

Graffiti cleanup programs, neighborhood watch programs, and neighborhood beautification programs can help to rid a neighborhood of gangs. They help give everyone in the community a sense of pride about where they live. They also help to make the neighborhood safer. If there are no such programs in your area, see what you can do to start them.

Help the Kids

It's a lot easier to keep kids from joining gangs than it is to get them out of gangs. Yet, especially in neighborhoods where there is a lot of gang activity, it takes a strong young person to resist the pressure from gangs.

Think about the reasons many young people are attracted to gangs—low self-esteem, the need for a family or a role model, and the need for a group to belong to. In some areas, kids say there's nothing to do for fun and excitement but join a gang.

Is there any way you could help these kids? Could you serve as a big brother or sister? Maybe you could help to start an after-school club for younger children, one in which they can learn to work together and support one another. Maybe you could tutor them or get them to work on a neighborhood improvement project.

Chances are, there are people in your area doing some of these things already. Check out the library, the Y, the schools, and the local churches to see what they have to offer. Talk with the police and probation departments. Often they have a youth outreach bureau that has programs for young people. Also find out if there are youth groups, such as the Boys' and Girls' Clubs, or programs sponsored by the city youth service agency. Then join in and help the kids—and help yourself.

CHAPTER 7

Staying Out and Getting Out

Q I've been in a gang since I was 12, but I'm grown up now and I have a kid. I want to get out of the gang. How do I turn my life around?

A At some point, things that you once saw as fun—such as beating people or breaking into homes—become less fun, don't they? As you grow up, you begin to understand the effects of what you've been doing. You think about how you'd feel if you were the victim of gang crimes. You get tired of the violence and tired of running from the police. You decide you want a future for yourself.

Good for you for choosing to get out! You're one of the lucky ones because you're getting out of the gang alive. It sounds as if you are getting out before a drug problem or criminal record destroys your chance for a future.

• • • • • • • • • • • •

Although it may sound surprising, a good place to turn is to the police. Many cities and counties have youth officers whose job is to counsel young people and help them leave gang life. The officer in your area—possibly someone you've always seen as your enemy—may turn out to be a very good friend. That officer knows what your life has been like and can offer strong support. He or she may be able to help you get out of the gang, finish school if you haven't done so, and find a job. If the police can't help you directly, they can probably point you toward others in your community who can.

Don't be afraid to turn to your family for help, too. Tell them how you feel and what you want to do. For some people, the best way to get away from a gang safely is to move out of town. In a different city or state, you can start fresh. Do you have any relatives or family friends who might be willing to help you get started in a new place?

When you leave the gang, keep in mind that you will have to begin building a new life. The "real world" is very different from the world you've been involved in. You're going to have to make many adjustments, and you won't have your familiar support system—the gang—to help you.

Fortunately, there are others who are waiting to help you. There are church, community, and government programs designed to support young people like you who want to turn their lives around. They will make your new life much easier, and you'll soon have a strong new support system in place.

Getting out will be hard, but it's worth it. If you were tough enough to join a gang, you are certainly tough enough to get yourself out.

Staying Out

The best way to get out of a gang, of course, is not to join in the first place. Many young people spend time with gangs but aren't really gang members. If you're in that situation, it's not too late to turn things around.

This is true even if you have been in trouble with the law. The legal system treats children less harshly than it treats adults. Also, no matter what your age, the punishment for your first illegal act is likely to be much lighter than for your second or third. While committing any crime is serious, and may end up on a permanent record, it doesn't have to lock you into a life of crime.

If you've been hanging out with a gang and want to stop, just do it. Get off the streets. Concentrate on your schoolwork and do extra work. Join an after-school club. Spend time in the library. Get a job if you can. The idea is to keep yourself too busy to hang out.

You can also make new friends. Spend your time with young people who haven't been with the gang. Remember, many teenagers are attracted to gangs and are tempted to join, but most make the decision to stay away.

Getting Out

If you have been a gang member for a while, you may think you've ruined your life forever. You may have dropped out of school. You probably have a criminal record. Even if you wanted to leave, you know how difficult that's going to be. Many people reach this point and think that it's probably easier just to stay with the gang than to get out.

What does it mean to stay with the gang? The penalties for the crimes you commit will get harsher and harsher. The more fights you are in, the more likely you are to get seriously injured, disabled, or killed. Many gang members become drug or alcohol abusers. It's said that the average age of gang members is 17—because most die before they reach age 22.

Some gang members say that the only way out is to die. Some even think about killing themselves. But the bravest are those who decide to work toward a future they can live with. It can be done—people are leaving gangs every day. Most go on to raise families, get good jobs, and live long, productive lives.

Jumping Out

As painful as it may be to join a gang, it's much harder to leave. Most gang members don't like to see others leave the gang. Some gangs will let you go, but first they make you go through a "jumping out." Like the jumping in, the jumping out is usually a serious beating by the other members. Generally, however, it is much more violent than the jumping-in beating.

Other gangs have different rules. "They told me I was a member for life and there's no way out," Anna said. "They told me that if I wasn't around when they wanted me, they'd come looking for me. If they couldn't find me, they said, they'd find my little brother or my mom. They didn't care who they had to hurt. I belonged to them." Another gang member said that the only way to get out of his gang alive is to get hurt so badly that you're in a wheelchair and no longer useful to the gang.

Fading Out

When Mick was 17, he decided to leave the gang. "But I knew what they'd do if I said anything. I'd seen what happened to other homeboys who'd tried to leave." So he went a different way—he faded away. "I never made any kind of official announcement that I was out. I just stopped hanging out with the gang—didn't go to their parties, didn't show as often as I used to. In time, they sort of forgot about me—and I was safely out of their activities."

Many ex-gang members say that Mick's way—fading slowly out of gang life—is the safest way to get out of the gang.

Life After Gangs

There is life after gang membership. It's a struggle to get there, but many people have done it—and they say it's worth it.

Practical Matters

The first thing to do is to plan for your future. Many gang members spend so much time on the streets that they drop out of school. If you have dropped out, think about finishing your education.

Most colleges and employers recognize the GED test as the equivalent of passing the requirements for a high school diploma.

If you're young enough, you may be able to go back to public school. If you're older, you can take a test and get your GED, which stands for General Educational Development test, or sometimes as the General Equivalency Diploma. It will help you qualify for a better job.

If you have finished school, you need to decide what to do next. Are you ready to get a job? Do you need some training? Do you need to join a drug rehabilitation program? Where will you live? How will you manage financially?

You have many questions to answer. It will take time for you to make plans and begin rebuilding your life. Set some realistic goals for yourself and—this is important—work with others who can help you meet them.

Emotional Matters

Schools, job centers, and the police can help you tackle some of your practical challenges, but they may be less helpful with the emotional challenges you face. As you leave your gang behind, you're going to feel anger, loneliness, sadness, frustration, and depression. All of these feelings can overwhelm you quickly if you don't turn to others for help.

There are many people in your community who are willing to help you. Why do they want to help? Some want to because they care about you personally. Others want to just because they don't want another gang member in their neighborhood. Ask someone from a local drug rehabilitation center, counseling center, or church to meet with you. Tell them you want to take control of your life—and show them you're sincere.

Some people, such as Leo, are reluctant to turn to others for help. He says, "I promised my probation officer I'd go into the community counseling center, although I expected it to be a waste. I figured, what do these people know? Turns out, nothing I told them surprised them or scared them. They'd heard it all before. The guy I met with was used to working with gang members. He'd been one himself. He knew exactly what I was going through. He even told me what I could expect to happen. And he was absolutely right. It was great—I could be honest with him, and he was direct and honest with me."

Social Matters

When you leave your gang behind, you need to replace it with new friends and new activities. The more you do, the easier your new life will be. Look around you—are there organized sports teams you'd like to join or competitions you can take part in? Maybe there are causes you'd like to work for. In one program in Albuquerque, New Mexico, ex-gang members help to feed the homeless in the city. Those who volunteer for this program say that being able to help other people is great for their self-esteem.

Many cities now offer midnight basketball games. Through these games, ex-gang members have a chance to challenge each other in healthy competition. For those with artistic or creative talents, there are mural-painting programs, youth newspapers, radio shows, and even literary journals written for and by young people.

Some ex-gang members join community protection groups. Since they know better than most people what it's like on the streets, these teens can be very useful in law enforcement. The best-known group of this type is the Guardian Angels. Around the country, members of the Guardian Angels patrol subways, streets, and parks. Quite often their presence alone is enough to keep areas safe.

The Guardian Angels were established in 1979 when founder Curtis Sliwa recruited New York City teenagers to patrol the streets and subway stations in their neighborhoods. The Guardian Angels now have chapters in the urban areas of Massachusetts, California, Illinois, Nevada, Texas, Oregon, Arizona, and other states plagued by gang violence.

Former gang members constitute a powerful force in reducing gang violence. These former gang members from Albuquerque, New Mexico, gave up gang life to form a rap band. They hope to succeed as rap artists and as positive role models for the youngsters in their community.

Share Your Experience

One of the best services you can do for your community is to help rid it of gang activities. You can make yourself and your community stronger by working with local younger kids. Tell them what gang life is like. Tell them what gang members do. Explain how hard it is to leave a gang once you join. Perhaps you can keep others from making the same mistakes you made, or almost made.

Where to Go for Help

There are many national organizations that can help you learn more about gangs—several of them are listed below. However, for the most accurate information, you should get in touch with local organizations. Local groups can tell you better than anyone else what's happening in your neighborhood. To find these groups, look in your telephone book for agencies sponsored by your city or county or by a local religious, civic, or youth organization. Check the yellow pages and blue pages under Counseling, Social Services, or Human Services. Also, ask your school counselor to help you find the assistance you need.

National Organizations

Boys and Girls Clubs of America
771 First Avenue
New York, NY 10017
(212) 351-5900

Community Youth Gang
  Services
5300 South Vermont Avenue
Los Angeles, CA 90037
(213) 971-8373

Family Service America
11700 Lake Park Drive
Milwaukee, WI 53224
(800) 221-3726

The Fifth Ward Enrichment
  Program
4014 Market Street, Suite 105
Houston, TX 77020
(713) 229-8353

The Guardian Angels
982 E. 89th Street
Brooklyn, NY 11236
(718) 649-2607

National Association of Town
  Watch
P.O. Box 303
Wynwood, PA 19096
(215) 649-7055

National Center for Juvenile
  Justice
701 Forbes Avenue
Pittsburgh, PA 15219
(412) 227-6950

National Crime Prevention
  Council
733 15th Street NW, Suite 540
Washington, DC 20005
(202) 466-6272

National Urban League
500 East 62nd Street
New York, NY 10002
(212) 310-9000

Parents Resource Institute for
    Drug Education (PRIDE)
The Hurt Building
50 Hurt Plaza, Suite 210
Atlanta, GA 30303
(800) 241-7946

Teens Against
    Drugs/Community Outreach
    Program
7040 West Palmetto Park Road,
    Suite 305
Boca Raton, FL 33433
(407) 391-3895

Youth Force
3 West 29th Street
New York, NY 10001
(212) 684-6767

Hot Lines

Children's Aid Society (Canada)
(613) 733-0670

Community Information and
    Referral Services
(800) 352-3792

National Runaway Switchboard
(800) 621-4000

The Nineline
(800) 999-9999

Youth Crisis Hotline
(800) 448-4663

Youth Services Bureau (Canada)
(613) 729-1000

For More Information

Young Adult Books on Gangs

Barden, Renardo. *Gangs*. Crestwood House, 1989.

Gardner, Sandra. *Street Gangs in America*. Franklin Watts, 1992.

Greenberg, Keith Elliot. *Out of the Gang*. Lerner, 1992.

Lang, Susan S. *Teen Violence*. Franklin Watts, 1991.

Webb, Margot. *Coping with Street Gangs*. Rosen Publishing, 1992.

Other Books on Gangs

Bing, Léon. *Do or Die*. HarperCollins, 1991.

Campbell, Ann. *Girls in the Gang*. Raytheon Company, 1984.

Dolan, Edward F., and Shan Finney. *Youth Gangs*. Simon and Schuster, 1984.

Hagedorn, John M. *People and Folks*. Lake View Press, 1988.

Jackson, Robert K., and Wesley D. McBride. *Understanding Street Gangs*. Custom Publishing Co., 1986.

Knox, George. *An Introduction to Gangs*. Vanda Vere, 1991.

Monroe, Sylvester, and Peter Goldman. *Brothers*. Ballantine, 1988.

Rodriguez, Luis. *Always Running, La Vida Loca: Gang Days in L.A.* Curbstone Press, 1993.

VHS Video Programs and Movies

American Me, 1992.

Boyz 'N the Hood, 1991.

Colors, 1988.

"A Catalyst for Action," Community Youth Gang Services, Los Angeles, California.

"Crime File: Drugs, Youth Gangs," National Institute of Justice, Rockville, Maryland, 1990.

"Gangs, Move 'em out of Your Life," Ontario Police Department, Ontario, California, 1989.

INDEX